An Astronaut's LIFE

T0044848

Working in SPACE

by Martha E. H. Rustad

CAPSTONE PRESS
a capstone imprint

Pebble Plus is published by Capstone Press,
1710 Roe Crest Drive, North Mankato, Minnesota 56003
www.mycapstone.com

Library of Congress Cataloging-in-Publication data is available on the Library of Congress website.
ISBN 978-1-5157-9820-0 (library binding)
ISBN 978-1-5157-9824-8 (paperback)
ISBN 978-1-5157-9828-6 (eBook PDF)

Editorial Credits

Abby Colich, editor; Kyle Grenz, designer; Tracy Cummins, media researcher;
Kathy McColley, production specialist

Photo Credits

NASA Multimedia: 19; NASA Image and Video Library; Cover, 5, 7, 9, 11, 13, 15, 17; Shutterstock:
Aphelleon, Design Element, d1sk, Back Cover, Design Element, iurii, 21, Zakharchuk, Design
Element

Note to Parents and Teachers

The An Astronaut's Life set supports science standards related to space. This book describes and
illustrates jobs in space. The images support early readers in understanding the text. The repetition
of words and phrases helps early readers learn new words. This book also introduces early readers
to subject-specific vocabulary words, which are defined in the Glossary section. Early readers may
need assistance to read some words and to use the Table of Contents, Glossary, Read More,
Internet Sites, Critical Thinking Questions, and Index sections of the book.

Printed in the United States   5960

Table of Contents

Space Jobs

Think of working at a job.

At this job you grow plants.

You care for mice. You fix machines too.

And you wear a space suit!

Astronauts do all these things and more.

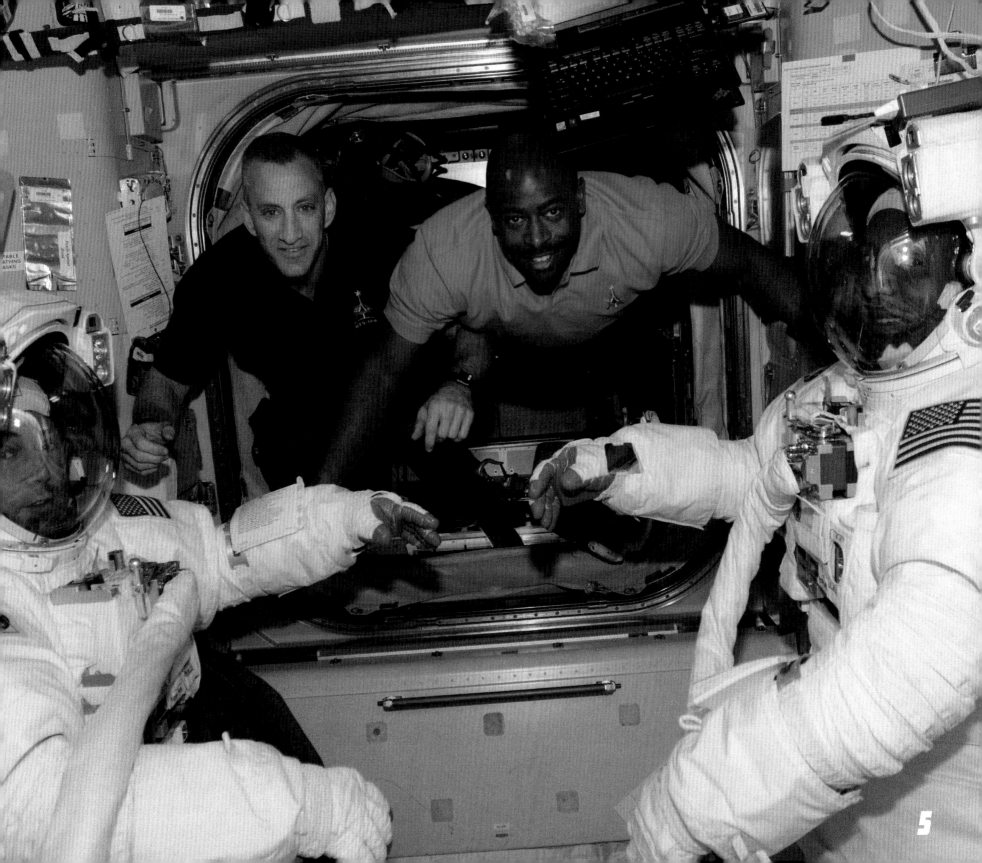

In space everyone has a job.

The commander is in charge of the crew.

Some astronauts are pilots.

They fly the spacecraft.

Other astronauts are in charge of supplies.

Caring for the Spacecraft

Astronauts care for all the spacecraft parts. They fix things that break. They must keep everything clean. Dirt can harm the equipment.

Spacecraft may need repairs
on the outside. Astronauts go on
space walks. They wear space suits.
Space suits keep them safe.
Twist! Turn! They fix the broken parts.

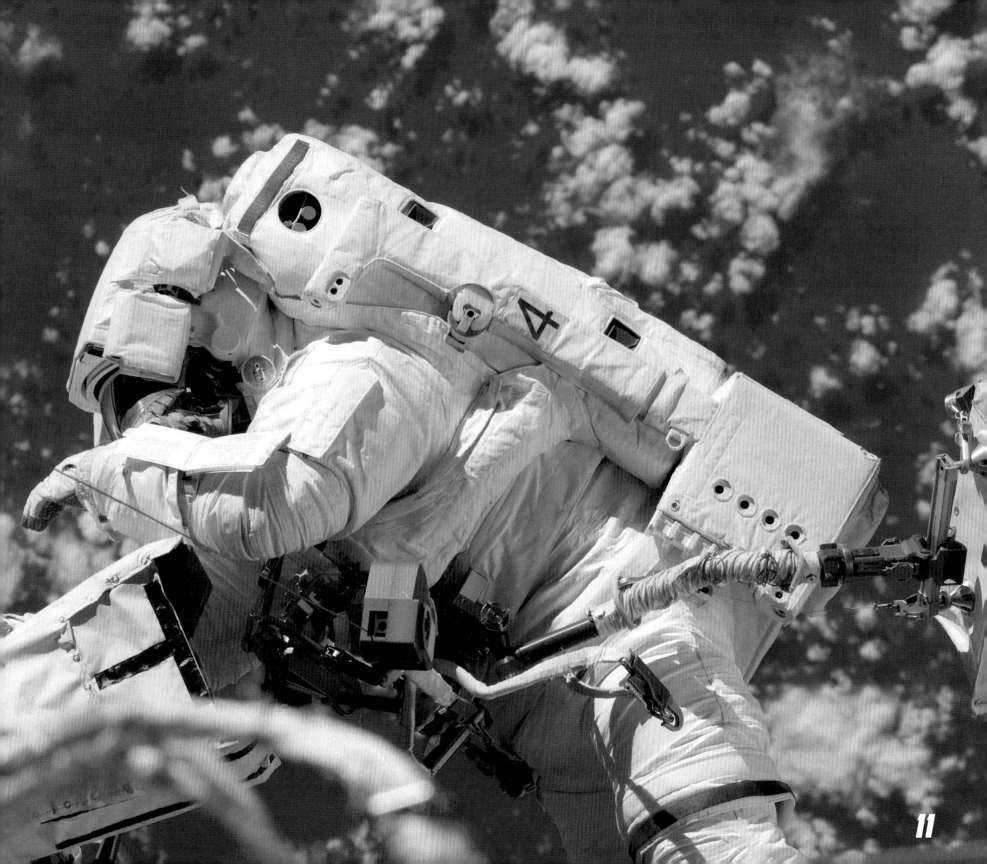

Experiments

Astronauts do experiments. In space, there is less gravity. Less gravity makes living things change. Astronauts study these changes.

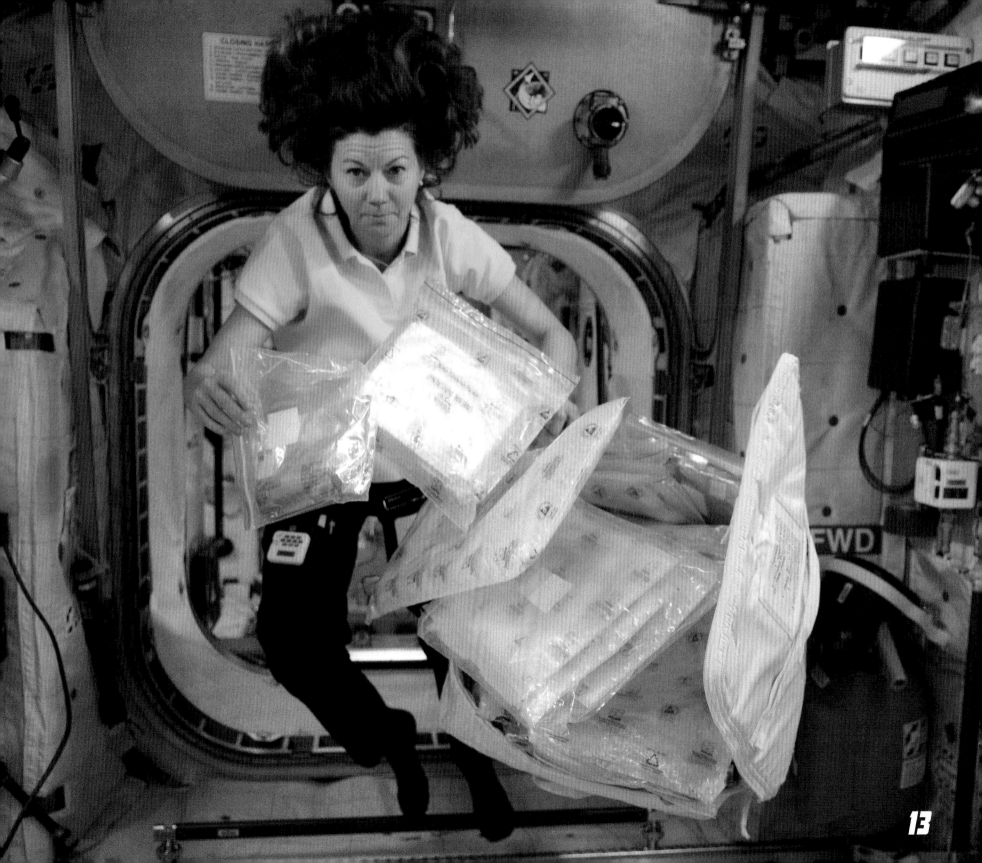

Mice, fish, and bugs have all gone to space. Astronauts care for these animals. They study how the animals change in space.

Astronauts study plants in space. They plant seeds. They water the plants. They may eat food that they grow.

Astronauts study themselves too!

They may stay in space a long time.

Their bones grow weaker. Their eyes change.

Studying these changes will help

others stay safe in space.

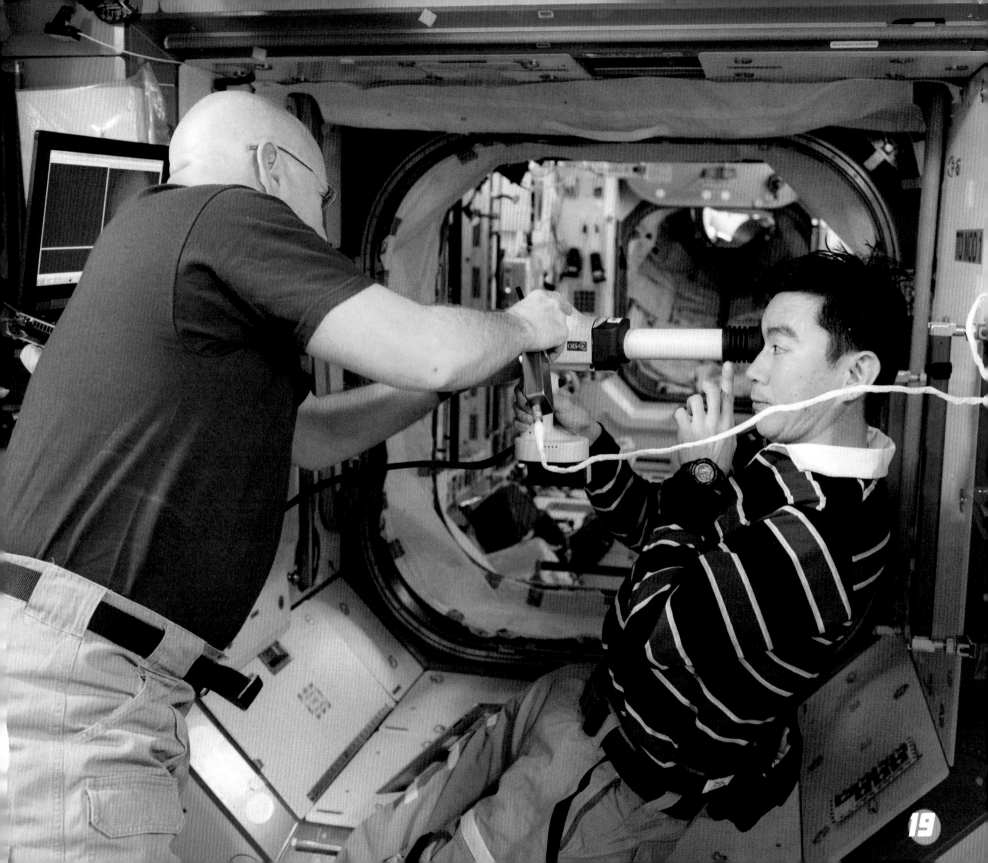

Future Jobs in Space

Soon astronauts may travel to another planet. They will look for life. Maybe you will have a job in space one day!

GLOSSARY

commander (kuh-MAN-duhr)—a person who leads a group of people

crew (KROO)—a team of people who work together

experiment (ik-SPEER-uh-muhnt)—a test to find out if something works

gravity (GRAV-uh-tee)—a force that pulls objects with mass together; gravity pulls objects down toward the center of Earth

space suit (SPAYSS SOOT)—a suit that keeps an astronaut warm in space

space walk (SPAYSS WAWK)—a period of time during which an astronaut leaves the spacecraft to move around in space

READ MORE

Gregory, Josh. *If You Were a Kid Docking at the International Space Station.* New York: Children's Press, 2018.

Owen, Ruth. *Astronaut: Life as a Scientist and Engineer in Space.* Get to Work with Science and Technology. New York: Ruby Tuesday, 2017.

Portman, Michael. *Why Do Astronauts Wear Spacesuits?* Space Mysteries. New York: Gareth Stevens, 2014.

INTERNET SITES

Use FactHound to find Internet sites related to this book.

Visit *www.facthound.com*

Just type in 9781515798200 and go.

Super-cool stuff! Check out projects, games and lots more at **www.capstonekids.com**

CRITICAL THINKING QUESTIONS

1. Name two jobs astronauts can have in space.

2. Reread page 6. Use the glossary on page 22 to find the meaning of the word "crew."

3. What do you think might happen to an astronaut who did not wear a space suit during a space walk?

INDEX